Straight and Curvy, Meek and Nervy

More about Antonyms

In memory of Hallie Nanda, mother
of Sanjay and Kavita. With gratitude
for her support of education.

—B.P.C.

Antonym:
A word that means
the opposite of
another word

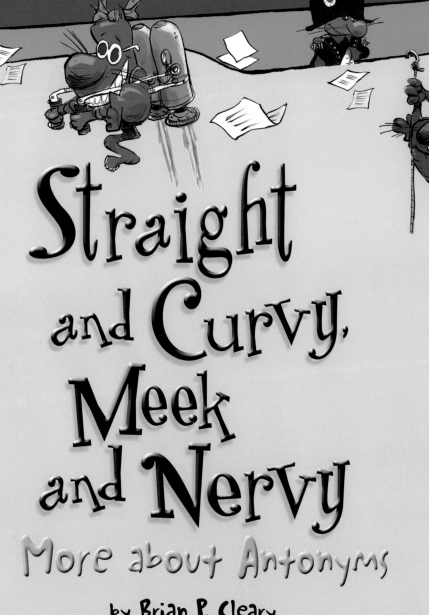

Straight
and Curvy,
Meek
and Nervy

More about Antonyms

by Brian P. Cleary

illustrations by Brian Gable

M Millbrook Press / Minneapolis

Antonyms are words that are quite opposite in meaning,

like sleep and wake

or give
and take—

like messing is
to cleaning.

Cheer and jeer are antonyms,

like straight and extra curvy.

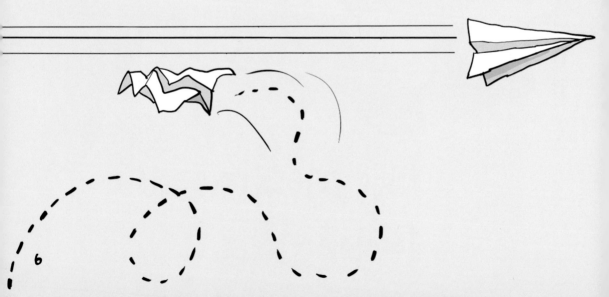

Wet and dry, and sell and buy,

as well

as meek

and nervy.

Drop and hold are also antonyms because they speak

of opposites, like stand

and sit

or strong

and somewhat weak.

If antonyms did not exist, we wouldn't have the words

to say, "I'd like the quiet— not the noisy— types of birds."

Or "Mrs. Scott prefers
when we are **serious, not silly**."

Or "The road in San Francisco

isn't flat, but rather hilly."

and you'll create an antonym—
let's try it now with

MIS!

ANTONYM FACTORY

As in a word like

MISPRONOUNCE,

MISTRUST.

MISSPELLED,

MISMATCHED —

each word becomes an antonym
with this prefix attached!

Sometimes putting

or

or often

18

before a word will make
an antonym—

shall we begin?

Antisocial, antilock, and even antifreeze.

Irregular, illogical,

and inequalities.

out and in are antonyms

and so are neat and messy,

shallow,

deep,

and lose and keep,

informal and quite dressy.

They point out major differences,

like **rainy** versus **sunny,**

healthy,

sick,

sluggish,

quick,

or grim and kind of funny.

Plump and thin are antonyms,

like spotless is to dirty.

real to fake,

and make
to break,

like bashful is to flirty.

27

They offer rich contrasting words
that help us to distinguish
day from night

and **wrong** from **right**—
and brighten up our English!

So, what is an antonym?

Do you know?

Find activities, games, and more at
www.brianpcleary.com

ABOUT THE AUTHOR & ILLUSTRATOR

BRIAN P. CLEARY is the author of the best-selling Words Are CATegorical© series, the Math Is CATegorical© series, the Adventures in Memory™ series, and the Sounds Like Reading™ series. He is also the author of The Laugh Stand: Adventures in Humor, Peanut Butter and Jellyfishes: A Very Silly Alphabet Book, and two poetry books. Mr. Cleary lives in Cleveland, Ohio.

BRIAN GABLE is the illustrator of several Words Are CATegorical© books, as well as the Math Is CATegorical© series. Mr. Gable also works as a political cartoonist for the Globe and Mail newspaper in Toronto, Canada, where he lives with his children.

Text copyright © 2009 by Brian P. Cleary
Illustrations copyright © 2009 by Lerner Publishing Group, Inc.

Millbrook Press
A division of Lerner Publishing Group, Inc.
241 First Avenue North
Minneapolis, MN 55401 U.S.A.

Website address: www.lernerbooks.com

Library of Congress Cataloging-in-Publication Data

Cleary, Brian P., 1959—
     Straight and curvy, meek and nervy : more about antonyms / by Brian P. Cleary ; illustrated by Brian Gable.
          p.   cm. — (Words are CATegorical)
     ISBN 978—0—8225—7878—9 (lib. bdg. : alk. paper)
     1. English language—Synonyms and antonyms—Juvenile literature. 2. Vocabulary—Juvenile literature.
  I. Gable, Brian, 1949— II. Title.
  PE1591.C54 2009
  428.1—dc22   2007052117

Manufactured in the United States of America
1 2 3 4 5 6 — JR — 14 13 12 11 10 09